# SPIDERS

# WOLF SPIDERS

## James E. Gerholdt
### ABDO & Daughters

Published by Abdo & Daughters, 4940 Viking Drive, Suite 622, Edina, Minnesota 55435.

Library bound edition distributed by Rockbottom Books, Pentagon Tower, P.O. Box 36036, Minneapolis, Minnesota 55435.

Cover Photo credit: Peter Arnold, Inc.
Interior Photo credits: Peter Arnold, Inc. pages 5, 9, 11, 13, 17, 21
James Gerholdt pages 7, 15, 19

**Edited by Julie Berg**

**Library of Congress Cataloging-in-Publication Data**

Gerholdt. James E., 1943
    Wolf spiders / James E. Gerholdt.
    p. cm. — (Spiders)
Includes bibliographical references and index.
ISBN 1-56239-510-6
1. Wolf spiders—Juvenile literature. [1. Wolf spiders. 2. Spiders.] I. Title.
II. Series: Gerholdt, James E., 1943- Spiders.
QL458.42.L9G47      1995
595.4'4—dc20

                                  95-12657
                                            CIP
                                            AC

### About the Author

Jim Gerholdt has been studying reptiles and amphibians for more than 40 years. He has presented lectures and displays throughout the state of Minnesota for 9 years. He is a founding member of the Minnesota Herpetological Society and is active in conservation issues involving reptiles and amphibians in India and Aruba, as well as Minnesota.

Revised Edition 2002

# Contents

# WOLF SPIDERS

Wolf spiders belong to one of the 84 spider families. A spider is an **arachnid**. It has two body parts and eight legs. All arachnids are **arthropods**. Their skeletons are on the outside of their bodies. Wolf spiders are also **ectothermic**. They get their body temperature from the **environment**.

There are about 37,000 **species** of spiders in the world. About 3,000 of these are wolf spiders. They are found all over the world.

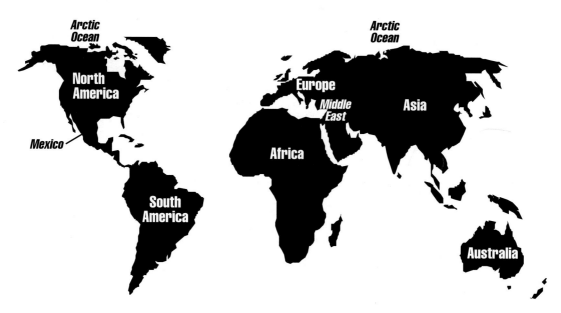

***Wolf spiders are found all over the world.***

Most of the spiders found in the Arctic and on high mountains are wolf spiders. About 200 **species** are found north of Mexico. They are small to medium-sized spiders with excellent eyesight that hunt on the ground.

# SIZES

Wolf spiders are small to medium-sized spiders. They are among the largest of the true spiders. They range in size from 1/5 (5 mm) to 1 1/2 inches (3.8 cm) long. Most of the **species** are about 1/2 (13 mm) to 1 inch (2.5 cm) in length.

The largest of all the wolf spiders found in North America is the Carolina wolf spider. This species reaches a length of 1 3/8 inches (35 mm) and is found throughout the United States and southern Canada. The forest wolf spider from the United States and Canada only reaches a length of 1/2 inch (13 mm).

**The largest wolf spider found in the United States is the Carolina wolf spider.**

# SHAPES

Wolf spiders may be heavy bodied or slender, depending on the **species**. They have two body parts that may be round, oval, or long in shape. The head and **thorax** make up the front body part, called the **cephalothorax**. The rear body part is called the **abdomen**, where the **spinnerets** are found. The spinnerets make the spider's silk.

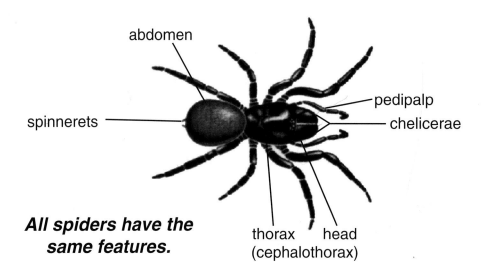

abdomen

spinnerets

pedipalp

chelicerae

thorax (cephalothorax)

head

**_All spiders have the same features._**

*This wolf spider is stretching out on a leaf.*

There are eight long legs attached to the front of the body. There are three tiny claws on the tip of each leg. Spiders also have a pair of **pedipalps**, which are used to grab their **prey**. The fangs are attached to the **chelicerae**.

# COLORS

Wolf spiders are usually brown and gray. Some **species** have interesting patterns that help them blend in with their **habitat**. This is called **camouflage**.

The forest wolf spider has two black stripes on its tan **abdomen** and gray **cephalothorax**. The legs are also tan. The burrowing wolf spider from the eastern United States has a gray or sand colored body with black speckles. The thin-legged wolf spiders are often a solid black color with markings on the abdomen.

*Wolf spiders are brown and gray
with interesting patterns.*

# WHERE THEY LIVE

Wolf spiders are found in many different **habitats**. Most of their time is spent on the ground. Wolf spiders are common. They can be seen running on the ground and over rocks.

Most **species** don't climb plants, but the rabid wolf spider from the United States is often found on low **shrubs**. Some wolf spiders live in sandy and wooded areas, grassy fields and meadows.

Most wolf spiders hide under rocks. Some may dig **burrows**. Others, like the forest wolf spider, use no shelter at all.

*Wolf spiders spend most of their time on the ground.*

# SENSES

Wolf spiders have the same five senses as humans. Like most of the spiders, they have eight eyes. Four of these eyes are large. Their eyesight is good, but not as good as the jumping spiders'. Since most of the **species** are active during the day, their vision is very important to them.

Other wolf spiders are active at night. You can find them by looking outside with a flashlight. The reflection from the spiders' eyes makes them easy to see. Wolf spiders also have a good sense of touch. It helps them find their way in the dark.

*You can see the large eyes on this Colorado wolf spider.*

# DEFENSE

Wolf spiders use **camouflage** to defend themselves against their enemies. This means their fancy patterns and colors help them blend in with the surroundings.

The **burrowing** wolf spider hides in its burrow, which may be several feet (1 m) deep. The pirate wolf spider from Europe lives in **marshes**. It builds a silken tube below the water level. When it is threatened, the spider retreats down the tube until the enemy is gone.

Other wolf spiders have no shelter. They use their speed to escape their enemies.

*Wolf spiders blend with their surroundings, which helps them avoid enemies. This female is defending her young as she carries them on her back.*

# FOOD

Wolf spiders hunt well. Because they have good eyesight, the spiders can see their **prey** and chase it down. They can spot prey from a distance of about one foot (30 cm).

The wolf spider will **stalk** the prey, then race forward and grab it. After killing it, the spider eats its meal.

The **burrowing** wolf spider will hide in its burrow until an insect passes by. Then it will leap out and grab its prey.

*This Colorado wolf spider is stalking its cricket dinner.*

# BABIES

Wolf spiders are good parents. The babies hatch from eggs that have been laid by the female. They are laid in an egg case that she has built for them, and will guard against enemies.

The egg case is attached to the female at the tip of the **abdomen**. She carries it until it is time for the eggs to hatch. She then bites the egg case open, and the baby spiders climb onto her back. If they fall off, they climb her legs and rejoin the others. After about a week, they drop off and go their own way.

*A wolf spider with an egg case.*

# GLOSSARY

**Abdomen** (AB-do-men) - The rear body part of an arthropod.

**Arachnid** (uh-RAK-nid) - An arthropod with two body parts and eight legs.

**Arthropod** (ARTH-row-pod) - An animal with its skeleton on the outside of its body.

**Burrow** - A hole dug in the ground by an animal; also, to dig a burrow.

**Camouflage** (CAM-a-flaj) - The ability to blend in with the surroundings.

**Cephalothorax** (seff-uh-low-THOR-ax) - The front body part of an arachnid.

**Chelicerae** (kel-ISS-err-eye) - The leg-like organs of a spider that have fangs attached to them.

**Ectothermic** (ek-toe-THERM-ik) - Regulating body temperature from an outside source.

**Environment** (en-VI-ron-ment) - Surroundings in which an animal lives.

**Family** (FAM-i-lee) - A grouping of animals.

**Habitat** (HAB-uh-tat) - An area in which an animal lives.

**Marsh** - A lowland covered at times by water.

**Pedipalps** (PED-uh-palps) - The two long sense organs on the head of an arachnid.

**Prey** - Animals that are eaten by other animals.

**Shrubs** - Woody plants that are smaller than a tree and have many branches.

**Species** (SPEE-seas) - A kind or type.

**Spinnerets** (spin-er-ETS) - The two body parts attached to the abdomen of a spider where the silk comes from.

**Stalk** - To hunt.

**Thorax** (THORE-axe) - Part of the front body part of an arachnid.

# BIBLIOGRAPHY

Levi, Herbert W. and Lorna E. *Spiders and Their Kin.* Golden Press, 1990.

Milne, Lorus and Margery. *The Audubon Society Field Guide to North American Insects and Spiders.* Alfred A. Knopf, 1980.

O'Toole, Christopher (editor). *The Encyclopedia of Insects.* Facts On File, Inc., 1986.

Preston-Mafham, Rod and Ken. *Spiders of the World.* Facts On File, Inc., 1984.

# Index